**Developing Reader** titles are ideal for children who are confidently using their phonics knowledge and can read short, simple sentences with only a little help. Frequently repeated words help improve fluency and confidence.

## Special features:

Short, simple s

Frequent repetition of main words and phrases

Careful match between text and pictures

Large, clear type

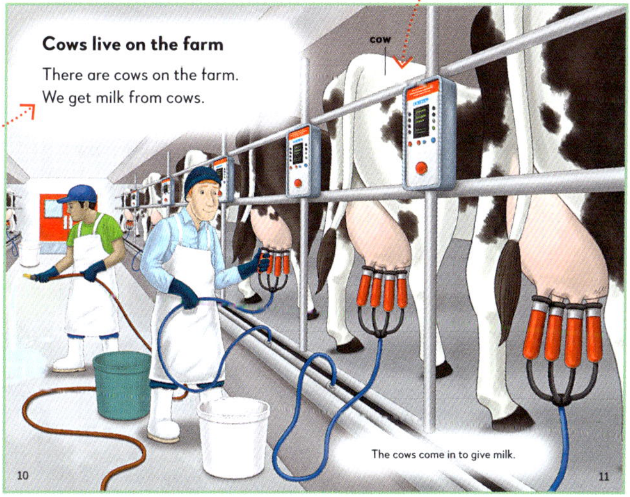

Ladybird

Educational Consultants: Geraldine Taylor and James Clements
Book Banding Consultant: Kate Ruttle
Subject Consultant: Dr Kim Dennis-Bryan

LADYBIRD BOOKS

UK | USA | Canada | Ireland | Australia
India | New Zealand | South Africa

Ladybird Books is part of the Penguin Random House group of companies whose addresses can be found at global.penguinrandomhouse.com.

www.penguin.co.uk www.puffin.co.uk www.ladybird.co.uk

Penguin Random House UK

First published 2016
This edition published 2024
002

Written by Catherine Baker

Illustrations by Dan Green


Printed in Dubai

The authorized representative in the EEA is Penguin Random House Ireland, Morrison Chambers, 32 Nassau Street, Dublin D02 YH68

A CIP catalogue record for this book is available from the British Library

ISBN: 978-0-241-56406-6

All correspondence to:
Ladybird Books
Penguin Random House Children's
One Embassy Gardens, 8 Viaduct Gardens, London SW11 7BW

MIX
Paper | Supporting responsible forestry
FSC® C018179
FSC www.fsc.org

Read It Yourself

# On the Farm

Written by Catherine Baker
Illustrated by Dan Green

# Contents

# Farms are for you

We get food from farms.

Farmers look after these animals.

We get wool from these sheep.

Farmers grow crops and vegetables, too.

We get milk from these cows.

## Cows live on the farm

There are cows on the farm.
We get milk from cows.

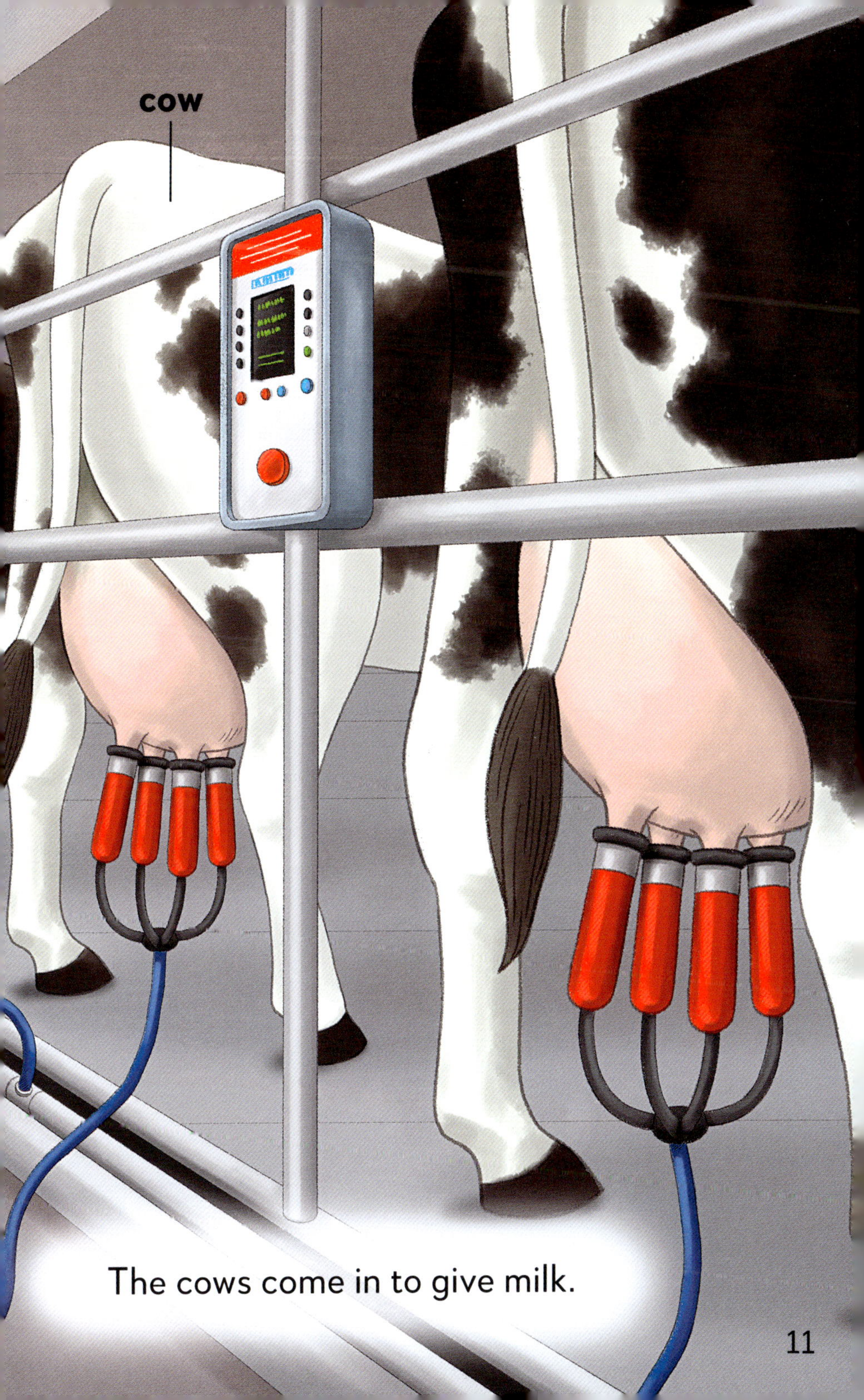


The cows come in to give milk.

# Sheep live on the farm

We get wool from sheep.

The sheepdog helps the farmer to look after them.

The sheepdog gathers up
the sheep for the farmer.

# Hens lay eggs

There are many hens on the farm. These hens lay eggs.

The farmer gathers the eggs.

# Baby animals

This farmer looks after the new lambs.

Baby sheep are called lambs.

This farmer looks after the very new calves, too.

Baby cows are called calves.

# Crops on the farm

Many farmers grow wheat on their farms.

Vegetables and other crops are grown on this farm, too.

Wheat and vegetables are gathered at harvest time.

# Food from wheat

Many farmers grow wheat on their farms.

Bread and all these other foods come from wheat.

# Machines on the farm

Farmers have machines to help them.

This farmer goes all over the farm on the tractor.

This tractor helps the farmer
get food for the animals.

# More machines!

Machines help farmers harvest the crops.

Machines can help all over the farm.

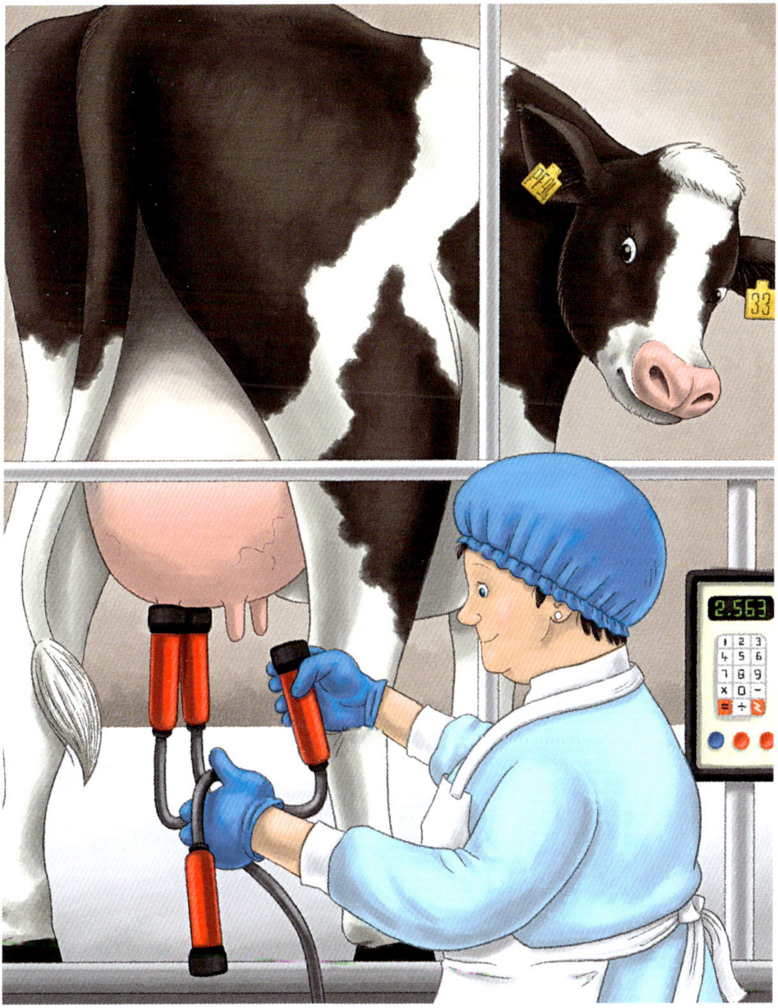


Some farmers have machines to get milk from their cows.

# Come to the farm

You can go to some farms to see their lambs and calves.

They are very little!

You can see the machines, too.

# Picture glossary

bread

calves

cow

eggs

farmer

hens

lamb

machines

sheep

tractor

vegetables

wheat

# Index